# Greatest Asian Poetry VIII

Contact Details

For inquiries, feedback, use of poetry, events, opportunities, invitations and more:

Please use the following email address to contact Aeon Julian:

AeonJulianLiterature@yahoo.com

‑

About The Illustrations And The Poetry

All illustrations and poetry in this book are original creations, by Aeon Julian.

The creation of the illustrations, comes from the foundation of spiritual belief in the Hindu depictions of divinity. In Christian religion there is a Divine Trinity, depicting, the father, the son, and the holy spirit. I, the author have faithfully resolved to trust the Hindu Divine Trinity most personally, including the Trimurti, and the Tridevi. The Tridevi is the feminine equal Divine Trinity to the masculine Trimurti. The Supreme Godhead and the Great Goddess are represented as being the incarnate of the energy that the three divine aspects indicate separately: creation, preservation, and destruction.

Throughout Greatest Asian Poetry VIII, the illustrations, including the feminine cover illustration, are included with descriptions.

The introduction of this poetry includes aspects of the author's life that have been significant in the creation of the poetry directly. Details that would indicate only fortunate aspects the author's life, are not appropriate to make a depiction of how the poetry came into creation. Therefore, the contentions from the author's life must be recognized to understand how the poetry came into creation.

No writing in the Introduction, Inspiration, Dedication, was written through the intention to propagate false events, beliefs, intentions, or depictions of any person. All writing in this poetry has been written through the acceptance and adventure of faithful purpose.

Sensuality is one of the main themes of the poetry. My spiritual alignment with Hinduism and Buddhism, especially elaborates the pursuit of spiritual liberalism. Individually, I believe sensuality to be of true creative potential and true creative empowerment. And in the poetry, I have made effort to elaborate that belief through individual faithful honor towards masculine, feminine spiritual equality. And also through the empowerment of the feminine through empowering the forms of their bodies, in opposition to the conservative religious adhering that includes prosecution of sensuality beyond procreation, and marital rule and law. This approach is individual, and is with the intention to elaborate feminine empowerment, in the illustrations and the poetry. Apart of my individual beliefs, is my opposition of the concept which celebrates virginity to restrict and promote against feminine sensuality beyond marriage, and stigmatizes sensuality into categories of oppressive unequal regulation. In essence, I favor sensual liberation, and maintain faithful morality standards in consideration of what I consider acceptable, and unacceptable sensuality. Ultimately, I'm opposed to making myself a rebel, black sheep, and minority, in my beliefs, and the east has spiritually accommodated a more outgoing and innovative approach, which aligns with my beliefs about sensuality. I can distinguish that my approach is one from a place aligned most with spiritual liberalism, Buddhism, and Hinduism. In ancient depictions of the Hindu deities, there were elaborated pursuits of sensuality, accomplishing sensual examples of spiritual liberation. Other themes included in this poetry includes: spirituality, morality, meditative, international, cultural, personal, and responding themes to feelings for the person the poetry is inspired by and dedicated to.

This book was initially entitled Vietnamese, Empowering The True Vietnamese Spirit. However, as the poetry developed into what it became, I realized that a less complex title was more suited and I chose Greatest Asian Poetry VIII, not with humble aspirations.

Every poem in this book revolves around Vietnamese spirituality, and directly, the person this poetry was inspired by.

Please take a moment to consider that all illustrations are not direct illustrations of Hindu deities directly, but of individual perceptions of a feminine divine trinity, and great goddess, with individual faith. And that is also apart of the inspiration and dedication of this book.

I proudly present:

Greatest Asian Poetry VIII

## Introduction, Inspiration, Dedication

To introduce this book, I must first distinguish the two names used in the title. 姬曨 (Ji Long), the Chinese name, is a self given name, which in English, translates to Consort Twilight. Chinese names often depict places, times of year, items, and similar. The surname 姬 (Ji), is a surname that dates to the Zhou Dynasty and the Yellow Emperor, and is one of the rarest surnames used in China due to the removal of Zhou surnames during the later Qin dynasty authority. To elaborate this choice of surname more: my birth year, 1988, is the year of the earth dragon, which matches the astrological animal and element of the Yellow Emperor also, the earth dragon. The animal and element has historical association with the most empire wielding significance among all the animals and elements in the eastern astrological charts. So I have taken the opportunity to give myself that decoration in my eastern name, as it was destiny that I would go there, and learn Mandarin (Chinese)

I chose the first name 曨 (Long), because that name depicts the connection between one state of being and another. It is the time of everyone's state of being, in which the earth turns from day into night, or the night turns into day and I consider that to be iconic of the spiritual destiny that includes the divine significance of incarnation, and eternal potential. The underlying significance that includes why I have included my Chinese name, will be included in the following paragraphs.

In 2008 I ventured to Dalian, Liaoning, learning Mandarin, self taught. And I realized far more identity with the east than I had realized previously. I remained there for seven months, remaining in a foreign languages school, after I effectively secretly departed from Los Angeles.

The secret departure, was due to a contentious situation involving oppression my family had perpetrated to keep me going through school. In the autumn of 2004, at age fifteen, (sixteen in October of that year) in the second year of high school I did not continue attending for one year and five months, to pursue music and writing. It was my intention to pursue music and writing without the partial restrictions that school environments and homework induced, for it was my intention to atone the skill I had pursued and developed to fulfill my intentions towards very significant accomplishments. It was a choice of devotion and new awakening, for me, and although there was much opposition in the family, my pride soared.

A conspicuous turn of events resulted from a family divorce including a secret flight from Ireland, where my father lived. My mother and father had both become psychologically threatening, due to their resentment, and opposition of each other, and the living conditions that resulted from leaving Ireland, created dangerous and volatile family divide.

In Evanston, Illinois, my grandparents provided a studio apartment, with no bedrooms, or beds, in the suburb of Evanston for one year and eight months between the early summer of 2004 and December 2005. Little did I know then, the impact of psychological condition on the situation: obsessive compulsive personality on one side of the parenthood, and functioning alcoholism on the other. Although that is not to discredit the musical brilliance of my father, one of Irelands most infamous traditional musicians, or his support for me in my pursuit of artistry, or his effort to do his best in fatherhood.

The resolution to stop attending high school, was for me, filled with epic hope and optimism, but among the family, it was received with moral panic and interrogative prosecution. I feared psychologists, because psychology seemed like one of the weapons used during the divorce to attain child custody. In reaction to my resolution in 2004, my mother cried hysterically on few occasions, but throughout most of the days that I was not going to school she interrogated me with threats about basic resource use, and made false implications during her interrogative efforts that I was afraid to go to school, due to a learning disability, or that I was on drugs, or that I was bullied. But my heart was resolved, and I would not be moved by any amount of adult aggression to do otherwise. I had felt oppressed and offended due to the years of moving temporarily to three states, and five houses with the family and the cooling relationship that turned hostile between my mother and father. In Virginia, 2001 in the seventh grade, at age 12, I began writing fiction, and that would continue from then onwards.

In Chicago, after the secret flight from Ireland to avoid loosing custody of me, my sister, and brother, there were many months of violent social conflict and turbulence between me, and my mother. The conflict led to a fateful 911 call that my mother made, in a panic during one argument, and I was taken to a youth mental health division. And with the conjured up stories that my mother convinced herself of, including that I was hallucinating, on drugs, anger management, (I certainly did become infuriated on occasion, loosing patience for the constant oppressive, interrogative behavior and actions of my mother), learning disabilities, and more, the hospital in Chicago was not in my favor. My distrust for psychologists was very significant, because for a year until October, the month of the hospitalization, my mother failed in mediating between me, and one psychologist, because my mothers intentions only resounded in the setting, as did my fight against such control and oppression.

Within fifteen minutes in the first session in the mental health division, the psychologist gave me a review that included a question that my mental health may have been due to bi polar disorder. It was not a diagnosis, but due to my reluctance to talk about anything due to distrust, he resolved that I should take medication throughout one year visiting him every month, attend school again, and within a year, he would confirm whether or not I really had any mental health problem. After three weeks, and my leave, his plan never developed beyond the power that my mother had to threaten medication in the case that I did not go to school. It was mostly a very interesting experience, to get to know in person what sorts of people were going into that health unit for three weeks total. I was frightened on occasion however by some of the events, like the break downs that some patients had.

It was return to high school on medicine and checkups, or a boot camp school in Utah! And my mother was prepared to send me there! It was a new beginning for me, because I knew that I could not use the same approach to success that I had used from 2004 – 2005.

I secretly avoided about a year and a half worth of medicine use, but for a few months I was made to use it through the implicative actions of my mother, that I would attend high school and use the medicine, or she would call the police to attempt enforcing me again. The enforcement was made to dilute the medicine and, I was watched to drink it. I knew that I could fight that… but that seemed too empty a pursuit… Success was my intention, so I realized that I too needed to understand behavior, or I would only encounter the rough.

Had I only known then that she had obsessive compulsive personality symptoms, then the entire ordeal may have been easier for me during then. But I considered such controlling and manipulative behavior to be evil, and only evil. I remained for a time, with sentiments that psychology must surely include the will of adults to have power through the power of the mind, like the dark side, attempting to control other people's minds, through inducing fear, and then making prescriptions to reduce the fear among the frightened. A person with Obsessive Compulsive Personality symptoms will effectively put fear to use to have control in relationships, as frightening as that is. Eventually I learned how to counter such behavior successfully, through understanding the symptoms more. It started to feel natural like knowing how to use self defense. And once the skill is perfected in self defense, perpetration of abusive behavior and actions reaches a minimum... In 2006 until 2011 I would not pursue psychology, so I did remain vulnerable to psychological threats until 2011.

After the departure from Chicago in December 2005, to Los Angeles... in 2007, the year I finished high school, I met a faithful friend who would help me to make a life changing resolution. I kept contact with that friend for several months, and on the night of new years eve, at 12:45 AM, 2007 - 2008, I departed for Beijing from Los Angeles, after convincing my family that I was going to a big new years eve party.

It was an enormous relief to be taking my efforts against the oppression as far as I could, and feeling truly cared for, for who I truly was, and that I was getting a truly fortunate international opportunity to be in a new environment. By the time of late 2007, I was ready to let one life be over, and to let a new life begin... I was prepared to not return, because my family had let their human rights status drop too low towards me. In late 2007, the pressure was on to go through college, and my family assumed that I was taking the medicine, after failing to follow up with the business-is-business psychologist in Chicago 2005.

I felt localized with the people in Dalian. I realized that from early on in my journey, eastern culture had been far closer to me than I realized. I felt spiritually liberated to be with people I could share the same feelings with, about spirituality on a local level. The martial arts, and Buddhist enlightenment had inspired me from early on, but Dalian provided me a new medium for my spirituality and spiritual beliefs to develop, and fortunately for me, to be in Dalian meant that I had the right resources to empower myself. I overcame one near deadly event in Dalian with newfound self confidence and esteem. Mostly, the festivals, restaurants, relationships, holidays, kept me feeling very significant connection to my hopes for myself.

It was a miraculous transition...

I succeeded in convincing my family to never attempt to use medicine again... Once they made their apologies and agreements not to, I left Dalian on July 31st for Los Angeles.

In Los Angeles, I continued pursuing artistry in writing and music as I had, in the underground fashion, not letting my family know because of personal distance in respected approaches between myself and the family. But, my family understood that I was not to be taken lightly in what I could, and could not do, and that did go in my favor. I avoided going through college for another two and a half years, through covert resolutions, and I pursued artistry individually, learned mandarin individually, and developed my spiritual beliefs during then...

After a contentious and traumatic event in September 2009, from getting mugged, and sacrificing my music player, which I used so often, to avoid getting assaulted from fists, blades or bullets… It was beside an alley during one of my lone walks. Unfortunately, more tragedy happened soon after. The family would move to a new apartment nearby, and during then, I would strain my right arm in three places after lifting too many heavy items without stretching and engaging in momentary horseplay with my younger brother. The immobilizing item that I ordered online was delayed a month, so the injury increased from a shoulder strain, to a triceps strain, to an elbow strain. I had gotten athletes foot on my left foot from temporarily wearing dirty substitute shoes the kitchen I was working at through summer, in the Yosemite Lodge, for I had applied to work there in early 2009. Under the tragic circumstances, my body was breaking, and throughout 2010, apart from the ten month lasting elbow strain, conflict with family reached near parallel to 2005. I felt self destructive, also, and new trauma resulted from this sequence of events, and endurances of those events. It was a duration I coined as ' The Roller Coaster Of Heaven And Hell' in my memos, from the paradise of Yosemite, to the hell of having my spirit feeling weighted and my bodies injuries, and the uphill progress during 2010.

My choice to enroll in massage school cleared me of the dire risks that would remain into late 2010. The family pressure ended, finally! And I had the opportunity to pursue healing, which I needed, from the traumatic impact between late 2009 and late 2010.

From August 2011, to March 2012, in Studio City, I graduated from massage school. I had some work opportunities, but I resolved after a few months of opportunity pursuit, to use personal fitness training for my interest in health and bodybuilding, for opportunity instead.

And so the inspiration for this book began.

In a case of right person, right place, right time, I met Vi Nguyen, a student of psychology in Los Angeles. She helped me throughout a year, overcoming the lasting risks that trauma would have over me. In the massage school I had resolved that understanding psychology would help me more than hurt me, and I considered what could be wrong in my situation psychologically, that did not include me. I had been interested in learning more since 2010, which I did, and my pursuit in psychology brought fate between myself and Vi Nguyen.

Instead of thinking about what my mother did as evil, and only evil, I considered what psychology could indicate, so that I would not remain bound to the mysteries of evil as being distinguished from everything else in the situation. So, I looked up online, what behavior included not knowing how to throw away things, controlling behavior, perfectionism, manipulative behavior, and I felt deep relief to understand that there was something beyond what I had already understood, that was at the source of some of the most significant contentions in the situation, which potentially impacted me.

I have used the understanding of O.C.P.D. to change the game, and I have avoided the continuing circumstance of being targeted for oppression and manipulation.

Having a certification in massage significantly reduced the oppressive and manipulative risks that I endured from 2005 through 2010.

However, there was a remaining risk, and that was trauma. I knew that trauma had impacted me, more than I felt was safe... Trauma had brought me to almost have very few panic attacks, during most stressful situations... And I felt self destructive too often... My sister had taken sides against me in every conflict, resulting in two vs. one, belligerent arguments, and I was on my own too often.

Vi Nguyen has been for me, someone that helped me recover through some of the lasting trauma. I wrote and developed techniques to overcome traumatic effects, how trauma induces the self to daydream more often to escape the stressful objectives, and such...

After reading into the war disasters of Southeast Asia, I realized that the United States had violated human rights and environmental standards against Vietnam.

So, I must make it clear that this poetry is greatest, because that is how I faithfully intended it, and this poetry is Asian, because the poetry revolves around Vietnamese spiritual empowerment, and it is VIII (8) because that is the amount of segments, and amount of poems per segment. And I consider VIII a faithfully divine number.
In terms of eternity, specifically...

I realized that people can do wrong things to support their power, and in the example of Vietnam, the United States took some very poor morality standards, in choosing how to reduce the risk of political power that the United States did not agree with.

My standpoint, is that just like the threat of medicine, to keep me in school, did have some impact on my body, including fifty pounds of weight gain temporarily... like the threat of warfare, similarly, that includes harm to nature itself, and the innocent is the threat that evil poses.

Evil, is a forbidden pursuit in a truly faithful, spiritual journey...

In Buddhism evil desire is to lack compassion and efficiency...

And it is a faithful journey that I live. I consider myself a faithful individual adherent to the teachings of the Hindu deities, the Buddha, and Jesus, particularly.

I resolved from my faithful development, from an individual place, that I can establish a true connection, between my self, and true Vietnamese spirituality.

I consider true spirituality to be the truthful incarnate of the self.

I feel sickened that even I feel frightened by the sort of sentiments that the United States has towards those who did what they did in good will, not to threaten the world with evil, or to cause disaster. Politically, I'm not making a point about my sentiments, but international individuality is to be respected, and that means not pursuing violation of those that favor other approaches to prosperity, or overlooking compensation for disastrous violations. In the example of Vietnam, the damages have affected millions indirectly, and that is historical fact. My faithful will is to promote compassion, and that's why the example has been included, so that readers will consider morality standards for the significance of divinity.

I consider writing this poetry as one of the choices I can make to empower truth among all good people, and places. And to make a promotive effort towards all true Vietnamese spirituality. I don't believe in overlooking true potential for the sake of political power, and I don't believe in only running from what I feel afraid of.

And so, in a public approach, this poetry is inspired by and dedicated towards empowering true Vietnamese spirituality.

However, this poetry was inspired by Vi Nguyen, and it is dedicated to her individually.

Vi Nguyen helped me understand how it feels to be a Vietnamese American.

She told me once that "The world is fucked up, and that's just the way it is," to depict her view of life. (The words may not be exact, but it was the same significance)

But, I realized that it was her experience. And I wrote this poetry in the hopes of giving people like her, who would feel that way in general, a more fortunate perspective to have individually. It's not that easy for an innocent faithful person to understand what it's like to live and really feel like the world is fucked up, and that is just the way it is! I've never considered the world like that faithfully, so I assumed it Vi's words were only to deceive me, so that I would accept my insignificance...

It's too easy to look at every person the same way, and I believed that did apply to my relationship with Vi Nguyen.

Apart from that, I felt like she was under constant pressure to meet expectations, and it was to the point of inhumane treatment, self inflicted. With self conscious bluffing aside, a bullies victim can pretend it's ok until the victim has resolved self harm. And I do believe that Vi was innocent in some ways, but this poetry is my resolution to be the influence that I consider most true in how I consider my aspirations in consideration of Vi Nguyen.

Through peer pressure, innocently, people may try to be aggressive with other people, but they also feel overwhelmed by the same sort of aggression. And there were a few times that Vi told me that I frightened her, and I assumed that she was attempting to turn her nose up, as though attempting to outclass me. And I was so, so, convinced, so that did hurt my esteem!!!

Through meditation I realized that she was, actually frightened sometimes, because I was too aggressive to pursue what I believed in, and that she felt unconfident and overwhelmed...

To distinguish how I felt, would be to include that while I mastered creating expectations, a point of power for myself, that Vi Nguyen was doing her best to survive under the expectations that other people made. And I had to reach beyond my own understanding, from the understanding that it's easy to get what I want in some ways, to understanding that for those less privileged in money, or for those with short height for example, that it's anything but convenient for them to get what they want. And so when Vi was surviving to meet expectations, I was concerned with surviving through individual faithful beliefs, raising my standards so high that it's not easy for others not to look up, to perceive me.

And that is because I have developed defense approaches against adult egotism, power, manipulation, and oppression. Frightening elitism works effectively to keep people from trying to put me in my place, and that is from my personal experience.

Apart of my personal offering in thanks for all the compassion I've shared with Vi, and all the creative energy, I have to make constructive criticism also.

Famed feminine psychological health author Rachel Simmons depicted that it's when a girl cannot speak of her most painful feelings to someone significant in her life, that she feels most destructive from the impact of isolation. (not exact wording, elaborative reference)

Apart from that I felt a familial love towards Vi Nguyen and I felt like peer pressure gripped Vi in fear of too often, convincing her that there were no other options. And I know that denial is the preferred resolve of the ignorant in confrontation with the truth!

I would compare peer pressure to the example: women, and military abuses. The peer pressure may inspire the target to enact the peer pressure, or go along with it... submitting to it, and perpetrating it, which turns into guilt, and self destruction. That is what I did not want to ignore, in my relationship with Vi Nguyen. Certainly, she can turn the nose up, try to use the same tactic that she has been encouraged towards, depending on the situation with her school, but I too felt interested by that same school, and it is only my concern that for someone like Vi, that opportunities will be too limited. That is based on my own interest, and the news about the lawsuit concerning the American Psychology Association and work opportunities. Then again, a rich person can turn up their nose, and live their life spending money carelessly, pursuing belligerent snobbery. Or a person can aspire to live like that, looking down and shunning anyone that resembles poverty in any way. And worse, delight in the pain inflicted upon others. Enforcing belligerent rules for selfish, and evil aligned self empowerment, and the temporary reliefs and power highs through abusive confrontations with those that idealize honesty, individuality, and liberation.

But, I want to make an example that is unlike that sort of perpetration, and I'm willing to oppose anyone that threatens to undermine me in doing so. And the reputational halt in the relationship certainly did threaten to undermine what I believed was faithfully true. So this book is to carry out a fight against that sort of threat, personally and in general: the threat that belittles, and degrades faithful potential, for the sake of financial power, and scholarly reputation, for example. I will not let such selfish perversions undermine what I have believed in, and the love I have felt for the Vi Nguyen that I have believed in also! And to make myself clear, I will fight it out until I'm the last person standing, even if I fall down more than once!

I'm certain that anyone concerned with the educational significance of my writing can view the information online in a search for psychology colleges in Los Angeles.

I was heartbroken that such a fortunate relationship could be resolved with destruction, and I felt inspired to give a new medium to the energy of the relationship, so that it would not be lost through the defeat of my faithful will... I felt that I had been making faithful choices, and to let what is alike with peer pressure defeat me spiritually was not faithfully acceptable.

An example of how status can be harmful includes the story I watched recently on American news about a girl who wore designer clothes, and she made fun of a girl that wore cheap clothes; hating her, belittling her. And then her mother was told about it, and the girl that wore designer clothes was made to wear cheap clothes to school, and she then did not make such cruel gestures. The turmoil the girl without the money endured was not deserved, and it was nice to see how the other girl chose a new attitude about respect and recognition afterwards...

My most significant concern was that fear would turn into destructiveness, and I knew that Vi was used to fearing high expectations from what she told me about how she felt...

I don't let evil have power over me, and that is why I'm not moved by some of it's more daunting potentials. The law that should be, for example, is not always the law that truth influences. The United States military is an isolated example of that in some of the risks that women soldiers have been exposed to. And that is not to overlook my sentiments about the freedom that the United States military has promoted in general.

I feel like Vi Nguyen did not have the confidence I had, and this poetry is to promote confidence, to be individual, not bound to reputation, and money, in whatever she could, through true devotion accomplish.

And that is my thanks for what she did to help me. In deed, I'm not going to let a halted relationship stop me, from celebrating that relationship, and letting everyone know how it has inspired me. Faithful resolution has guided my choice to write this poetry, and no confrontation will overwhelm me into keeping my individuality censored and regulated!

And in a personal and direct statement:

It has taken me months, and I do believe that unless you can accept truth enough into your heart that you will not let censorship and regulation dominate your choices, that this poetry certainly shall carry on the progress I made with you...

This book is also inspired by and dedicated to anyone that understands what it means to live for truth, not for reputation, and not for money, in most significant ideals... This book is to inspire the will to accept and pursue salvation, over selfish intentions over others.

And in the highest honor, this poetry is to honor the potential of true love, and divine truths.

I pray thee bless thy light, not curse thy darkness!

- Aeon Julian

| 14 21

Romantic Dawn
The Night Dragons Fate
A Divine Offering Underlying Wisdom
Status Spitefulness
The Lost
Instead Of Conditions
The Rich Excuse
Without Consequence

|| 22 29

Sensation Of The Sky
True Pride
Striptease
Duel
Protesting Cruelty
Hardcore
The Kiss Of Fate
Game Of Failure

||| 31 38

True Benefit
Another Side
Vietnamese Appreciation
Elixir
Divine Reality
Written Portrait Of Jesus Christ
Unknown Essence
Divinity Threatened

|V 39 46

Sensual Fantasy
Shamans Wisdom
Technology And The Spirit
Celestial Fantasies
Beyond One Earth
Enslaved Spirituality
Little Girl Anthem
Like An Orphanage

V  48 55

Divine Medicine
Ascending The Boundary
Natural Fortune
Masculine Authority
A New Earth Fantasy
Deities Story
Divine Kingdom Verse
Ascended Will

VI  56 63

Liberated Awareness
True Vietnamese Spirituality
Shrouded By Mystery
Fallen Spirit Requiem
Inferiority Complex
Only Human
Hiding From God
I Am The Truth

VII  65 72

Beloved Eternally
Thyself
Thy Requiem
Supernatural Soul
Beyond Devastation
Empowering
Enlightened Awakening
Inner Peacefulness

VIII  73 80

Sensuality Storm
The Feminine Resolution
Violence
Rape Fantasy
Capsaicin
Alluring The True Alignments
Southeastern Sensuality Royal
Vietnamese

Notes About The Author  82

The Great Goddess, aligned with Hindu supreme goddess, the Mahadevi by Aeon Julian

## Romantic Dawn

On a chilled, permeated, dense cloudy morning, her silken eyelids opened,
Smiling at the effluvium clouds, sighing at the night vanquished blue,
She arcanely insinuated against sleeping on the grass, although it was implied,
In the opulent, moist grass, in the efflorescing garden,
Adjoining the cascade mountain bluff diagonals,
In the natural underworld, the northeastern Pacific Rim, a mesa of volcanoes,
The energy of the earth lusty, vigorous, a monster fire dragons sanctuary,
She had sprinkled, sprayed, and spurted, to water it,
The cleavage, the grass, the garden plush, loaded...
Surrounded: a verge, of appraised stonework,
Intramural to her adorned home, her bosoms desired spruce design,
The decorations measureless, blanched, russet,
And she contracted the limit of her wet, transparent, white gown,
As though it were only from the fleeting water tickles through the starlight theatre,
She thought of, her daughter and her son,
Both asleep in their rooms,
She breathed fathomlessly,
Each of her buxomly bosoms tightened and love stained...
Looking up, a hot sweat beaded and dripped from her face and rich scalp,
Around her suave, golden, ecru ankle, her little white undergarment,
Against the soles of her bare feet, were his,
They remained motionless,
Their breath became unfluctuating again,
Their slumber had only seemed...
His unripe green irises, surrounding his night dark pupils ogled jubilantly upwards,
His spiritual fortune glissaded from her pale lavender sensual inlet, swollen still,
With her fingers clenching it to her silk supreme lips, for her insubordinate tongue...
He thought about it for a moment...
The uncivilized, vicious rain like her love overflowing all over, again and again...

## The Night Dragon Fate

An aphotic dragon would sojourn to perch, outside in the nebulous nighttide,
So nebulous the peacefulness, tarrying for some vehement violence to trigger...
Perched on the parapet of a dwelling quarter,
The orphic incarnate of a lethiferous fortune,
As though comatose, crystal, veiled with caliginous eclipse,
Quiescent, slumbering, halcyon,
Beside her house, on a dry soil street, a drunken Vietnamese girl induced,
Drinking with a sordid friend she considered incorrupt,
Aggressive, not the surface mien,
A yielding delivery,
And then become inebriated,
So was she...
Ceded, despondent,
She quenched herself, amassing,
In a somber glazed daze,
He actualized to fight,
Arguing her makeup a violation,
That the other men would favor her,
He was Vietnamese besides,
In a meager suburb,
In a northwestern American desert region coastal city...
She could not argue to score, because she was too muddled...
He was three times her perimeters,
From abaft he retained her in his arms vice,
Too hard, she blubbered quietly, in absent disquietude,
Squirming, elbowing, running like a startled little girl,
He pursued awkwardly, catching seizing her left right arm,
And swung her around, until she tottered into mud, hands, face, and knees,
Beginning to sob,
As she sobbed, he lifted her, and furiously jabbed her in the stomach,
She vomited... choked... hung in the air by her arm in his clench... unable to breathe...
Pillaging and plundering her clothes, thrown again into the mud,
The aphotic dragon roused... energized...
Some masculine stranger, on an exalted, carousel night returning home,
Did keep his military sickle ripper,
Once all of her clothes, her perpetrator removed, and she was bare, unclothed,
And her rapist penetrated her front from behind,
The masculine stranger stared at them for a moment,
He smiled as crookedly as the occurrence!
"I have a knife..." he spoke quietly into the gusts and gales of hot night air,
Within a consternated moment, as the drunken, bare girl cacophonously yowled, choking,
A flash fast blade sunk once, into the upper left back of the rapist... his heart bled...
The heroic vigilante wiped his blade on the dying rapist's clothes... evanishing away...

A Divine Offering Underlying Wisdom

To accept such wisdom,

" The foolish assume their fate objectively,
Bound to obscurity,
Obscurity to spirituality,
Those that pursue power ignorantly,
Will collapse through power,
Living in spiritual suffering,
An example: an apple, stabbed in one place,
So that left outside,
All insects would pursue,
All of the sugar fermenting,
Until an entire part of the apple would become brown,
Isn't that how some spirits are?
Like beggars for divinity, with nothingness produced for higher fate,
When will they become whole again?
Looking back… with regret… that they did not know…
How that would happen,
Violation…
The seemingly vanished tainting,
Remaining…
Living only with what they have,
Unconfident about divinity…
Playing wrongful games too often…
Overlooking truth…
Like a wave… rising up… only to fall…
Uniform with everyone,
It would seem,
As though it were everything…"

To accept such wisdom…
To accept such faith underlying…

Status Spitefulness

Some girls are addicted to glamour, excusing it as passion, aspiration,
There are those addicted to status, faithlessly so,
Desperately so... ignorantly...
Their spirits are consumed with small groups of ideality,
And the world in their eyes is small,
For they perceive a small reality.
' Each person has a role,
And they follow it with loyalty,'
Overlooking faith... all and every... one with impoverishment mostly,
Those so addicted to glamour... see glamour... and glamour only...
Spiteful of faith... spiteful of divinity...
For in their ignorant eyes... divinity is vanity!
And towards truth they consider not,
Addicted to candy, in a candy store, fascinated!
Unknowing,
So selfish, with majorities, incompatibility!
Resentfulness, destructiveness,
As the self revolving self lusts against faith,
Evil lusts the self revolving self,
Through thy knowing, destruction predetermined,
Those so blind, their minds eye... taking and keeping, until they fall,
Blind judgments, for favorability...
Spiteful against all material alike to poverty,
Desperate... so much that...
For money the self accepts spiritual and bodily rape,
The violent forms,
And the ignorant, so addicted to money,
Descend into obscurity, to save face,
Hiding the violations...
Inviting, and refusing...

The Lost

" I've pursued you... to stalk you... to violate you...
I'm guilty so punish me... beat me for taking you...
Punish me for touching what I should not have...
Punish me when you cannot move from this brutality...
When you're frozen... like you've been assaulted and taken from...
Numb emotionally... punish me...
I will punish you more,
It seemed that was our story, like you were too ignorant to understand me,
And for it you villainized me until you could blame me for all your upset,
A little girl having a tantrum,
So lost in lascivious ignorance,
That you hate whoever cares the most, the most..
In your violence, will you turn on yourself?
Will you not point the blade at your self,
Because you feel so out of control and fallen,
Small, small feelings, so big up close,"

'Is that how she felt,'

I would wonder,

'Could I not penetrate the layers of insecurity?
Or would it only amount to more upset,'

For those that felt so lost..

Instead Of Conditions

" Isn't it so, that you felt guilty all along?
The one that lied to yourself,
Living it, in a life of mysteriousness,
I've wanted to know you but you wouldn't let me,
And I'm assuming then you didn't know yourself,
So you didn't know what you were doing,
It's too bad that you made me feel like,
The closer I got to you, the more wicked you would become,
Because you were cliqued with another group,
And you'd sacrifice truth for power,
Brutalizing me, breaking me down,
Just so that unless I was just like you, I would fall apart,
Some of my family have made me feel that way,
But I know there are those that kill who are not the same...
Maybe to an extent of abuse and devastation you're like that,

Would you have made me a prisoner? Would you have made me an offender?
Had I trusted that you would let me know you more than conservatively?

I didn't feel much doubt that you would have confronted me,
Until you severed my desire to be with you,
Did you think that you were that glorious?
Did you think I was so poor?
Is that how you decided that it would be ok to break me down?
Did the pressure of conformity give you that right?
To be accepted... to be acceptable...
Well then my darling...
You're only a little girl in spirit...
And because I'm compassionate,
I can only love you for what you really are...
Did you make a disgusting mess?
That's ok... I would have cleaned it up for you,
But you had a lot of power,
And I knew that doing that would have cost me...
So little girl, as foolish as you were...
Maybe there will be spirits a little more grown up,
That will use their power a little more carefully,
And then, maybe one day, you will have the courage,
To beg me for acceptance,
Enslave yourself to me for your impoverishment,
And for it there will be fortune...
Compassion is what you need to look for instead of conditions,
From now on..."

The Rich Excuse

" Poverty is one of the main mediums,
That provides for evil to become powerful,
So be wary of those so easily tempted...
Those so easily bound...
They will sever your state of mind,
Should you have individuality,
It will not remain unharmed...
One moment safe...
The next, targeted...
And many can threaten few...
Carefully in heart... carefully resolve...
Not to be so easily moved... by foolish groups...
So easily... from wealth to poverty...
The fool born into it can fall...
When you cry, you should still accept the truth... don't go about living a lie...
Just to protect only self revolving desires,
Yours or theirs,
One day,
That world would collapse,
And destruction consumes all of it,
So much that it happens to you,
That's the truth!"

Without Consequence

Enemies…
Isn't that like the choice between conservatism, and conflict?
For those so ignorant,
The bars must be so tempting to bend…
Like the opportunity to rape!
So willful to strip the clothes off of the body!
Should she refuse him,
He could beat her until she is too weak to move!
The enemies…
Could it be, that she wanted it so much,
That she challenged him to open her up?
To penetrate her… give her his fortune…
From within his body,
She would have went such a length,
To tempt him, she was so longing…
So pushing for the stimulation of destruction,
To inspire him, to penetrate,
And so desiring, the thrill of his striking intensity,
Deeper within than her fingers could reach,
And more powerful,
She too was longing to escape the bars,
For her desire was too convenient!
She needed faith in her resolution,
So that they could remain together not for consequence!
So young, her spirit, that she did not know,
And soon their relationship would end…
He would like a prisoner run…
And she would become a mother…
Crying to the heavens to help her!
' What has the world become…?' she would feel… sorrowfully…
Sorrowfully, had she entrusted her spirit to mine,
She would not assume only consequences,
Of her destiny… of true destiny…
And instead make truth intended sacrifices,
Less, the overwhelming influence of instinct…
' How I have wanted to penetrate her…'
To fulfill my passion without consequence…
Not only in body… her spirituality would surround mine…
The feminine and masculine fortunes… ascending…

## II

### Sensation Of The Sky

Walking on the clouds, white puffs, grand in lofty wind,
Air and water deities in spiritual forms,
Taking one form... then another...
Be it a resolute, storming cloud, in bottomless blue,
A colossal flock of crows,
A jumbo hawk,
Two human bodies in sphere like auras,
Pink, blue, red, black,
White light,
Tiptoeing, hopping, skipping, surging, on the highest clouds, so high up,
Diving, flying higher to a highest wisp, and to then remain, seated
Convinced!
Looking down to the tiny details of the lower clouds, lowest clouds,
Tiny below, so high,
Realizing that it was not so,
Falling, down, down, down, down,
Until waking up in a cold bedroom,
Snow had fallen from the night before,
From a cool evening, the windows open,
So cold outside of the bed, so insulated!

## True Pride

Strip them of their pride,
Remove faith in their culture,
Their history,
And make them a generic breed,
Like something acceptable,
To one empire, not more than one,
Give them one identity,
Without it, their confrontation,
Like slaves, sex slaves, sex tourism,
There are those among them,
Guilty of the same,
To lust the flaunting... empowers them...
They play the game of glamour,
Teasing, not giving,
Unless the material is offered in much amount,
Such a pathetic existence that would be,
So faithless, sexually objective,
How pathetic...
Such a pathetic racial group,
There must be so much more not revealed...
For the belligerence of one empire against it...
Let their women look pretty so that they are taken...
And let their men be weak so they are fallen...
The fire of truth burns so bright,
I'm not so ignorant that I shall not see...

## Striptease

The whore that teases…
She is too pretty to go near!
Too well off, too high in merit,
Seeking the most prosperous partners,
Lusting material fortunes,
Picking and choosing,
Spirituality primitive,
In her self conscious perceptions,
That frustrated me…
Because I wanted to care,
' Votes of no confidence,
Until there is material evidence,'
The only basis for her judgment,
No trust in the spirit,
How weak and inconsistent,
Not me… the whore that teases…

## Duel

However much I love the people,
And I want to be their champion,
I hate that there are those who seem to have the nerve,
To become so offended by anything less than absolute wealth,
That they associate everything offensive with any sort of poverty,
Including me,
So that I'm a threat to them...
Should I have wanted to help in any way...
That is unbelievable...
They want to see blood spill,
So that they can take! To take what they want...
A game of theft,
To steal money from the materially less victorious,
Through status accomplishment,
How disgusting! What is there to care about?
I've wanted to care... to realize they point their weapon...
At me...
I should point mine at them...
Kill or be killed?
Boasting compassion like money?
I will shoot first,
And I aim well...

## Protesting Cruelty

You may look beauteous on your outermost,
But you don't know how to intercourse!
You cannot release, and you don't know what that is!
So, you do what your parents want...
You wait until you get married...
You talk down to anyone that goes a little too far...
And you have your mean attitude!
You think you're sexy!
When all you do is show off!
And you don't even know how to stimulate your own breasts!
You wait until that day finally comes!
And you get married!
So... on the honey moon you have it...
But you are not skilled...
He comes too fast...
And you can't at all...
I wanted to be nice supremely,
But I realized how people like you would react...
So this is it, bitch,
People like you terrify me...
You feel under an offence?
I've felt like that many times...
I don't accept it...
But I'm really not upset...

I just wanted you to know I feel about you

Hardcore

I like it,
Holding your hips,
Feeling your legs around mine,

I like it,
Feeling your center saturating,
Listening to you cry in a high,

I like it,
Seeing sweat slide down your cheeks,
And feeling your tongue in my mouth,

I like it,
Feeling you swell up,
And come like a flash flood,

I like begging for it,
With my lips and my tongue,
Do you want it to, do you want me to come?

## The Kiss Of Fate

" Kiss me...

I want to play with your upper lip,
Sucking it, biting it,
Until it bleeds a little, and you shout,
I want to, bite your tongue so I can,
Capture more than I should want,
How swollen can I make your love?
How long can you be like that?
How long until I can drink your tears?
From your high, and how careful must I be,
To make you cry loudly, without coming,
Because once you do, it's over...

So... Kiss me...

Let me feel you around, until you are intense,
And you start coming down,
Shivering nervously, your heart beating fast...
Weakly, so high,
Let my fingers give you resolve,
And then you will not wonder why anymore,
Just like a new fate,
I will release all of your yearning within..."

## Game Of Failure

It's a game of failure,
To make purpose,
Being a player…
Having something over someone else,
Ardor… to hurt another… just to feel high,
All the time…
Not questioning magnanimity… although not accepting it…
Pursuing evil empowerment,
Not knowing what it means…
A game of failure,
The power system,
Not morality, not truth, not falsity,
Just power… status… and relief…
Ascending spirituality is not only about instinct,
Having something instead of not having something,
I wanted submission to faith..
But that seemed not to be the resolutions she made…
Ah… how divinity to some is not wise too!
I should sigh in the wind to know myself..

The Creator Goddess in sensual form, aligned with the Tridevi by Aeon Julian

|||

## True Benefit

Did you believe it was fair?
To let your mercy come in the form of public empathy?
And not any exclusive effort?
To let them not know that they were accepted?
Did power excuse the opportunity to turn the nose up?
And to overlook god as only apart of the church,
Is that how blinded by lust the government was?

So it seems…

I have not accepted such mental illness,
For those with their evil energy within, shall point their fingers,
Using whatever poisonous idea, perpetration,
Indication, attempting to taint the essences of truth,
Pointing the finger in some sickening accusation,
And then through a hidden evil sicken,
A contest of evil… how sick can they make their targeted…?
How mentally ill can they demote their opponents…?
And next… will they die like beasts in violence…?

One day

True divinity shall not keep mercy
Criminals against untold laws will not pray their way out of punishment
There will be truth for the spirits so true
And ascent for it

Another Side

Sub human...
Maybe that is the excuse,
Subtle evils,
Petty slights towards devilry,
Group bumping,
A little trifle closer to the edge...
Of the cliff...
Fall off...
It was a crimeless mistake,
No ones fault,
A little knock here,
A little knock there,
One knock, two knocks, three knocks, four,
Five knocks, six knocks, seven knocks more...
Maybe, a procrastinating game of kill or be killed,
Strike first or fall first,
What does it matter?
A little destruction throughout...
More and more...
And then... fall hard...
Intense... break down...
Fall sick...
Medicine poisoning...
Loving the opponent to death,
Twisted, bizarre, lost, falling,
Until a new phase of devastation,
From the other side,
Another side

Vietnamese Appreciation

How cruel, nobody seems to take responsibility,
The sheepish delights and thrills,
Of doing nothing,
Looking on…
That's not my breed, not my spirituality,
I'm not so easily conforming,
It hurts to see Vietnamese potential neglected,
Overlooked, disposed of,
Could it be that in the west their dragon-like traits,
Were associated with the devil?
And maybe from that spiritual ignorance,
Some moral panic gave right to war criminality?
I don't accept it,
Ecocide, genocide, is undeserved,
The first world country should not proudly, not recognize,
The reality of the acts,
It is no compassion to Vietnamese spirituality,
Like the reward for a good deed is tainted,
Not rightfully… how could I continue faithfully,
Overlooking how I feel?
I could not without compassion,
To provide them my perceptions, and resolutions,
Who would I be, unless I did that?
A person less than he used to be…

## Elixir

Where are their kings, their queens?
What fortunes have they to share?
From one progress to the next,
Taking that opportunity from them,
Hypocrisy, for freedoms protected,
Freedoms are destroyed,
Not the faithful destiny,
Under what country can authority become so... that is not a country corrupted,
To be foreign,
I cannot embody purity to know,
And not know faithful resolution...
The remedy of the spirit fallen...

## Divine Reality

There comes a duration, that heroism is questioned,
What is heroism, why is there heroism?
For who, and how is there heroism?
Had I questioned it, not the pressure of countrymen,
Family, or government would have dominated my resolution,
Despite who may question my choice,
Judge my act, I know faithful heroism,
Beyond the boundaries of ignorance,
My heroism, gives me unconditional wings,
Higher divinity provides me, my fate,
However I must depart with those under any evil influences,
I will… and my fate shall be true…
Joviality, and lull, shall underlie my choice and preference,
Not some, group domination…
A true warrior fights for truth… in truth…
Not using the flames, or toxins, that hell provides,
I care not to be judged by religious authorities…
Be it any member of any church… divinity is my authority…
Had the lord Christ a church to credit and discredit him?
I need not convincing through argument…
And I sing my song in writing,
The aligned with true divinity would know,
It is not a false world I have known…

## Written Portrait Of Jesus Christ

A devil could preach... segregation...
Of all sorts... remove spite with punishment...
The power of reputation... systematic authority...
To give the truly faithful all and every shortcoming...
In an age of science... they know not faith...
Undermine the every significance of religion...
As something of the past...
And consider not the ascent of faith itself...
That is the devils fate...
To avail Jesus for cultism...
And not the subtle lesson of his fate...
He measured his truth... that he accepted punishment... for others sins...
And his faithful intent... compassionate parable...
Not cultism... the power of evil again...
Complete absolutism... treasure and dominion...
It was not the motive of Jesus Christ...
In the faithless human world metamorphose...
Religious extremism arousing religious extremism....
Contumacy...
From one origin to another...
The descent of religious foundations...
True faith remaining beyond it...
As wild as the natural earth...
As unknown as truths influencing written words...

## Unknown Essence

An umbra, cloud veil sky remained... lolling over the mountainside...
Unripe green, altered to nubilous green, subaqueous brown and profound blue,
On the earth's lowest surface... slightly torrid... in the highest sky... arctic...
Tropic forest ridges...
Leaf and branch married silhouette...
Although hot and lush exotic allure...
The sky remained arctic highest... fair entwined white ornament elitism...
Ethereal vaporous...
Where highest nimbus claims aureola and corona gleefully...
Aloft and atop, overhead vicissitude green, felicity thy promised land for thy life,
Only the highest bowed and apical summits bargained frore offerings to thy beloved,
Below, thy incalescences for thy quality,
Oomph steam, oomph heat, replenishing thy most oomph exotic,
Resplendent... vivid passion... rich bloom... imbued impregnations...
Thy kernel... thy soul essences... thy marrow...
Pure exotic plenary... capital and meridian...
Zenithal fertile bountiful in thy lands lavish basins,
Where ocean essence frolicked and hustled with phosphorescent swards,
Thy raw sparkling... anew divine creation then...
Unknown essences... unlike faithful perceptions...
The cobalt, and beryl skies... hidden overcast ulterior... twinkling stars occult...

## Divinity Threatened

The substantial beast that wandered forth,
Through southeastern tropic jungle,
Could not know what animal resided,
In some region... arcane spirits...
In some unnoted form...
Unsung...
The plants perennial... Elixirs exotic...
Falling into paradise...
Another world... another fortune...
Without a shadow of evil pride...
The world is pure,
Whatever begins without end...
Continues...
Had thy known,
That devils made their mark,
Thy destruction unto them,
And evil designs resolved..

IV

## Sensual Fantasy

" Honeycomb, let me hypnotize and lure thee,
I will wrap you in the finest threads,
Until you cannot move,
Tickle you're bare feet until you cry,
So that you almost faint…
Until I coerce and dragoon your legs apart,
My sadism… amaranthine…
Had I not craved and fancied thee,
I would have nevermore yearned the opportunity,
To convince you I loved for this torturous intimacy,
Until you have become undone with pleasurable torture,"
I would not stop…
Be it my lips… my tongue… my teeth…
My fingers… whatever I need…
To undo your oneness…
So that you are spread…
So that I can rest within your energy…
You resist… and I persist…
Until you are too tired… to remain so wholesome…
And I can move your fingers for you…
With the defeat of your resistance…
I will not claim victory…
I want to feel your counteraction…
Your assault for my violation…
When you're too tired to make it harmful…

Shamans Wisdom

The great wood fires, come from the oldest wood,
Old for the mutations within,
Old for the decompositions that begin,
That is why the greatest wood fires,
Come from the oldest wood,
Flames would burn as though magic were its fuel,
Dancing about… colors unalike…
Shoots of fire… fire shoots…
Crackling…
Fine perfume…
How enlightening… the oldest wood… makes greater wood fires…
The flames seem to never stop burning…
And wood,
The oldest life on earth,
Gives power to flames,
Elixir of the stars,
Thy interaction is so… the plants and light are…
That light from fire… creates life…
And from wood to light, fire…

Technology And The Spirit

Technological nightmare,
Had it been the steel,
The walls,
The smoke that shrouded clouds,
Militarism that overwhelmed,
Destruction of life,
Tools of evil empowerment,
Dissecting the human,
Then it would not have been,
A technological nightmare...
All in a subtle breath,
I could perceive the reality of spiritual cancer,
Taking wrong directions,
Overlooking truth,
The result,
Only disease,
So doubtful of truth and falsity,
Divinity and evil,
To perceive the fate of the descending...
For a moment,
The intestines disturbed the body,
And in a frightening awakening,
Into darkness,
The sensations of waste...

Celestial Fantasies

Had humans been the only ones,
Could there not have been only one variant?
The wolf and not the tiger for ponderous example?
I've wondered such strangeness
Had earth never been visited,
Then, would firework fantasies, conspiracies, and propaganda be so openly used?
Considering the strange like that... it seems that some high ranks believe...
Disturbing the desire to oppose such strange things,
Could it be that propaganda must use natural reality to some amount,
And some contentious sorts of people are guilty,
Maybe enlightening to consider,
In a ponder of thy creations,
Thy animals of humanlike potential or never,
For humans have cultivated farms and founded national cultures,
To have faiths and religions,
For thy true fortune,
How can that be mistaken?
To consider how complex the beloved mammals become,
For example in strange ponder, the human, another similar animal,
Thy chimpanzee!
Another strange ponder, on another earth, it would not be misfortunate,
That among all things, humans were not so easily so...
Although, the concept was a little too daunting...
Unlike the ease of the human and the easy...
For my pondering, no evil empowerment
For only ascending truth should guide me
Without the pursuit of manipulation

Beyond One Earth

In martial arts, the opponents consider weaknesses,
And target them, to defeat the other opponent,
In the example of the gun vs. the bow,
There is a disadvantage,
Take the ever mysterious unidentified stories,
And conspiring,
Letting go of that, and government,
Any human group on earth,
Such unlikely fantasy,
Like a perception of something that would venture,
A hundred or five hundred octillion more miles through the universe,
And the consideration either
There is, or there is not, is pointless,
In the context of human potential,
In such unlikely fantasy
Should the day ever be that,
Like fantasies of wingships, fantasies of space transit,
A lesson of history this poem could be,
Like matcha green tea…
In the will of eternity

Enslaved Spirituality

Poor wisdom...

To allow for people to assume the worst...
To assume their defeat, their destruction...
To assume that, there is no victory...

That they are slaves
Slaves to those with authority
Slaves to systems
Slaves to habituality
Slaves to isolation
Slaves to family
Slaves
Too poor to assume truth
Too poor to assume beyond
Chaotic, samsaric
Mixed reactions, mixed beginnings
Mixed feelings, mixed ratings

That's the place of the spiritual slave...
Stuck in a chain reaction...
Until their worlds end...

## Little Girl Anthem

" How I love you!
Caring for you, every moment,
Not so easily considering,
That you're a foreign being,
Too foreign to understand,
Too poor to realize,
Compassion from enslavement,
So, I would hold your hand,
I would be your friend,
Giving you something to consider,
More than just an obscure ability,
Little girl, I should be your old man,
I would feed you right,
And give you space…
And so that you were not a spoiled brat,
Crying to have others accomplishments,
When your parents refused it, reflecting temptations not to,
In my eyes, you're more than that, super little hot shot,
Let me be your old man,
I'll teach you how to be true and pure,
Beyond a poor fate,
I want to carry you in my arms, and make you squeal in thrill,
Little girl, aren't I what you never had…?
Let me carry you away, far, far away…
And then, when you want…
You can go back…
With awareness you used to not have…"

## Like An Orphanage

In an orphanage,
A hundred children are...
With no parents to keep them safe...
The supervisors wait,
For them to sleep,
The noise is loud...
It can be a spiritless place...
Sad, empty, lonely,
That's the consequences of poverty,
Playing out with parentless children,
But me... I understand how they feel,
I don't overlook it,
I don't look down on it,
I understand,
There are those with families,
Out of place,
Feeling similar,
Those without countries,
Running away, from violence in the homeland,
Crimes and killings,
Drug money,
And the sacrifices of many bodies,
The orphanage... such an emotional hardship,
The children without parents,
Is it so contentious?
Once one child reaches beyond it?
They have a world to carry with them,
Without it, they are in the same contention,
So many others are in,
Walking without a family to walk home to,
But faithfully it would be so,
So I offer the wisdom directly...
Should you know truth... divine and pure truth... measure it...
And then know more...
So that your spirit ascends...
The boundaries of any contentious impoverishment...

The Preserver Goddess in spiritual pose, aligned with the Tridevi by Aeon Julian

V

Divine Medicine

Trauma
Loosing objectives
Holding on to the imagination
Running away, running away
And then, without running further away
The trauma catches up
Even though awake
A moment of daydreaming
With a nightmarish trait
So vividly
That it's like reality
For just a moment
A striking sensation
Like waking up from a nightmare
A pounding heart
Sweaty palms
Unable to escape
The continuing fear…
Something violent and destructive
Feeling it somehow in everything…
Sensations of terror
Things that are similar
The trauma caught up too much…
Panic attack
Running from the moment
Like a demon has found the self
Cannot get it out…
Feeling conflict within
The person that was, and the person that is
Imagination too powerful
Wanting to escape so much
Looking for a way
Spitefully
The blade…
The vein…
As though not reality
Stuck with a distant consciousness
Stuck, like defeat…
Until you win
You seem to keep loosing…

Ascending The Boundary

Although the colossal mesa sierras are too steep and formidable...

The heavens avow crystal fair, the greater venture thee...

The more energy you seem to spend...
The more benefit you seem to apprehend...

The precipice pyramids bequeath thee
Extravagant ardor greater

Than the devils that hunt you...

With you, wild animals give compassionate ardor also...
With holy promotion upon thee...
You need not feel overwhelmed...
Although understanding not
Sensations of fear
Eventually, most bizarre sensations
Come to be obvious to notice...
The state of being that felt eminently delicate
Shall harmonize to become powerful...
For submission to ascending truths
The plight circumstance of spiritual carnage resolved...

Higher divinity... will create you again...
Like divine spirituality created the stars...
You have the same potential...
It may be enduring...
But for it, your state of being is rewarding...
To you, and the ascending true realities...
So keep fighting, for truth...
Keep submitting to truth...
And eventually, confronting reality...
Will be locked up...
Like tyrannical criminals imprisoned...
Or, like an impatient spirit wiser...
The consequence of not looking one time...
The consequence of witnessing something...
How guilty it could feel...
As though you were punished by god...
You were not...

You were only too innocent to know bread from dirt

Natural Fortune

Fairy queen...

Vietnamese...

You know who you are
Dressed in briar vines and blossoms
After inviting a humble girl
Let me hear you crying it
How you feel?
Deep
Like you've only accepted
The swelling warm touch
Moving around
As though your smooth body, of the oceans brine

So saturating, your body...

Once I demanded from it enough...

As though like a dance
Got too close
Your mouth gives
Without words
And your center spills
Like a hot spring splashing
How passion becomes so exotic
In feature and flavor
Imagination and creation
Seemed to unite
For the taste I could never taste
The vision I could never truly enjoy
All from the creation we pursue
In our purest form

So it was...

Masculine Authority

From brother to brother
A lesson of masculinity
To hold absolute responsibility
Enforcing responsible authority
Maintaining morality
Offering such truth
Not evading it
It is the rightful form
Of the masculine
Understanding
That the larger body
Is not to manipulate
Protecting compassion
Yes...
Defining, and reducing it
No...
To resolve threats
Against the defenseless...
To hold accountable
Those that commit evil cabals...
Not to advocate them
From brother to brother
Only death is like a villain's partisan...

## A New Earth Fantasy

It would have been like a phenomenon,
To consider the earliest days,
Of this inhabitable earth,
When the first oceans combers and rippling tides,
When the first clouds in the teal celestial ceilings,
Light white huffs, puffs,
Through days and nights,
Remained,
When the first animals grew,
Had some rightful human like being felt,
To enjoy that,
Would we not all desire like to covet?
How blissful it would have been,
To see such a sight,
Similarly,
How blissful it would be,
Should the true opportunity become...
To perceive some inhabitable earth in some orbit,
Recently formed,
Where so early it was,
That no seeds were ancient,
For they were only new,
But in truth,
We should never pursue such fortunes,
Unless we were so desperate,
That our own earth was at some critical risk...
In this ponderous fantasy, to protect thy natures potential...
At least...

Deities Story

The autumn is glowing,
Copper, golden, chocolate,
Hard sugar candy shards, fall on apple green, iced grass,
Trees like cinnamon,
Clouds like cotton,
Forms become unfamiliar,
The long prelude of love anew,
And soon the winter will benumb,
The earth's amber and ochre,
Dormant green life,
And human life saved,
In sensual pursuit,
Heat against the coldest coldness,
And frozen snowfall,
To inspire spite for love again,
The frightening autumn prelude,
Influencing human life to pursue,
And in the winter war,
Love succeeds for victory,
As it is over,
The spring awakenings,
Plants, animals,
The deity's perceptions of reality,
To know the will of the seasons...

### Divine Kingdom Verse

' Bind me to your forms, I pray, divinity,
I have enslaved myself lone to thee,
For you can free my will,
I trust it completely,
Let me build fortunes, in your will, in glee,
For it is my spiritual choice,
I fear not the endurance,
I have submitted,
And I shall not flee,
I have trusted in you,
And that is my fate,
My will, to remain,
For thee, thy resolution, free and rightful,
For that is my intention,
It is not only my intention,
My purpose to pursue...
What indication have thee?
To provide me the road to thy kingdom,
Grant me the promotion!
And I shall find that road,
Without falling through descent,
The undivine empowerments,
That are unlike my pride,
So keep me in thine... true divinity, '

## Ascended Will

How hard pure air is to breathe,
Knowing the soreness within,
I'm happiest,
For my spiritual suffering is vanquished,
And my spiritual creation has prevailed,
I'm not bound to mistaken choices,
I have not mistaken will,
And so regardless of how enduring,
The pure air may sting, may dry, my crack,
The skin of my throat, my neck,
But I have no fear of it,
Grant me passage to thy kingdom,
And protect me against the doubt,
To turn around...
Half way up...
After I have prepared, again and again,
The fortunes that await me at the top of the climb,
Shall replenish me,
And not the fortune of my falling unworthy,
To where I have prepared for to arrive,
My fortune awaits me at the top of the climb,
And I have no intention to stop, through time,
No destruction mysterious, and powerful
Shall distract, or overcome me,
No doubtful indications, to overwhelm me,
For this duration, a super human, I shall become,
And divinity shall grant me entrance,
I have not intention not to ascend!!!

VI

Liberated Awareness

To not give up,
Is to understand divinity, more,
To choose convenience,
Is to understand it less,
With faith, giving up may seem right...
But it's not going too far sometimes...
Like an ornate colored, sand rock desert,
And knowing how to cross it...
Digging wide holes for holdings in the earliest mornings,
Sleeping through the day,
And hiking through the night,
In the cool, empty oceans subtle wind hypnotizing...
And divine sighs softly move...
For who had known that night was the time of the desert crossing?
Not the day!
Miraculous fortunes...
Pride shrouds in mystery...
Using starlight and moonlight,
Like a compass,
To provide the direction,
Locations of animals,
Needles of the cactus,
To slice it for aloe...
Although self defense...
An ascended offering...
Wisdom to the instinctive,
Contradicting...
To the spirits, liberated,
A fantasy map of the roads,
To the heavens!

True Vietnamese Spirituality

Backwards… a rebellion against all uniformity…
No size of body… or trend of politics…
Could influence the true Vietnamese spirituality…
Into the complex of devilry…
Forfeiting human life for systematic authority
The southern fox lives without captivity,
Some personality ideology falsity…
The trait of a self-over-divinity, political authority!
And the impoverishment of the people that live diversely…
No trend of popular culture to determine them,
Some tribe like reality only…
What is true Vietnamese spirituality?
Not some survival of the fittest…
Primitive human state of being!
And not the primitive aggression!
Poor patience, material addiction…
Having children to enjoy the most basic,
Living like that, and nothing more…
The false Vietnamese spirit is so…

### Shrouded By Mystery

Temperamental, that is what it seemed,
A short fuse, a quick delivery,
Resentful behavior,
Isn't that their impoverishment?
So impoverished, that formal displays of patience, ignites it,
Like a stupendous devolving,
How pathetic,
What accomplishments result?
None,
Obscurity,
Remaining,
What next?
Human trafficking,
Left to overcome hell...
Had there been some opportunity...
Some hope to rise from such falling...
Beyond international brides...
And modeling...
For rich foreigners pleasures,
Only still in obscurity,
Had there been some true fate...

Fallen Spirit Requiem

Lost in the hyperborean sky…
Over the snow, rock, blue Antarctica…
Lost… the spirit…
Broken,
Unmovable,
Motionless,
Unusable,
Naturally,
Restfully,
Not yet awakening…
Fallen to lifelessness…
Winds,
Coldness,
Nothing,
The Vietnamese reality…
In a land of the living…
The truth among them distant…
Frozen in the highest sky…
Untouched by human life…
Where stars glow in the darkness…
And the blue atmosphere receives sunlight…
Until a new fate…

Inferiority Complex

Some fortune of green...
Tropically...
The beat of the ocean wind...
Sighing and gusting...
Silencing...
Oceans waves...
Hatefully...
No reality beyond that...
For Vietnam...

Where is their culture?
Where are their fortunes?
Is there nothing of it?
And are they all just so the same?
Is that how they like it to seem?

Small and alike...

I hate to think... that is how it is

Only Human

Primitive woman…
In pursuit of copulation somehow,
Only human?
In pursuit of emotional interaction,
Only human?
Waiting for the opportunity,
To pursue some wild game of sex,
And considering that like romance,
Ignorant woman…
Finding the right man, really fast,
That's how to win,
It is so easy to let it all happen,
And do nothing more,
Only human?

Hiding From God

Any way to paradise…
Gamble, and feel high!
Do nothing, and feel tired…
Sleep and be nothingness…
And fade to become forgotten…
Fading from fortunes…
Becoming silent…
Once noisy,
Too easily broken…
And once falling,
Soon to crash…
Unable to make choices,
Depending on the easiest resources…
Whatever is local…
And too easy,
So easily hurt…
Depending on the basics…
Trying to make something out of it…
Feeling happy for the moment,
Making the highest feelings out of it…
But that way of living is too well hidden,

To well hidden from thee…

I Am The Truth

How sorrowful,
That I would forfeit,
Letting go of their true spiritual potential,
And pursuing only superiority,
Through the resolution, to turn the nose up,

" Who cares?
Who cares about them?
Those people,
There,
It doesn't mean anything,
Whether they are alive or not,"

That would be unfortunate,
How sorrowful,
Assuming their failure,
Intending only my victories,
In emotional domination,
Such ignorance…
That I would be too ignorant…
For then I would not be the truth!
The truth that is like clear water,
Is the truth that is like water worth drinking!
But there would be those to contest,
It does not matter how dirty the water is,
Because drinking is more worthwhile,
Similarly, money!
It doesn't matter how dirty the money is!
As long as there is money!

I am the truth…
And that is how "*you*" will know me…

The Warrior Goddess in wrathful pose, aligned with the Tridevi, by Aeon Julian

/||

Beloved Eternally

For ignorance is so,
That… for they are Vietnamese,
I shall not perceive them as worthy to notice,
To have the double standard,
To know them as those I can commit a second standard against,
Advantage taking…
For who cannot use the power,
To take what money can buy?
However disastrous,
Devils would claim,
No responsibility,
Without the careful care for politics,
As though human rights is money,
And money can be anything,

My faithful vow
To reach for those innocent of true compassion
To give them notice
So that those aligned, will know my place
Among the stars
And those aligned, will seek my spirit
Not unknowingly

Living as though they had never known my spirituality…
Blessed are those who ascend
To perceive through divine spiritual mediums
Apart of divine reality
Blessed are those who rise over ignorance
Be it in the forms that are so personal…
So reputational…
To not doubt truth for the moment
And the divine moments of progress

Beloved eternally

Thyself

For those in pursuit of power may love only themselves…
And not anyone else…
They are not beloved in divine nature,
Purest skies,
Highest mountains,
Greenest forests,
Most transparent oceans,
I know not any truth…
Unworthy of those places…
For those in pursuit of power do…
Starving and addicted,
Like instincts,
The reaction of the addiction…
Fallen human forms…
Looking for the fortunes…
So frightening
Perceive them not so collected and powerful,
However many those could seem…
As you are the minority,
You are not in only a minority…
For with your devotion… you are like…
The purest skies!
Highest mountains!
Greenest forests!
However least thy wind
Purest thy air
Know thyself
Beloved oneness
Beyond the state of, self-higher-than
Thyself
In divine alignments

## Thy Requiem

The end hath cometh,
Break thy enemy in two,
And break thy two enemies into four,
For thy victory,
The derelict city, evil, undone,
Hidden in thy creations,
Thy kingdom,
Thy embodiments,
Truly divine consciousness,
Fallen has thy bitter enemy,
The devil,
And then to know thy earth,
I walk higher esteemed,
Silenced by thy wind,
Thy blue, thy white,
And thy morning sunrise,
Thy night,
And thy night's freedoms,
Resting, awakening,
And thy stars glitter thy darkness
Silence...

Supernatural Soul

Here her body hath fallen,
Broken into pieces of crystal,
Once a body of a spirit,
From it, scattered crystals,
For she lived in misfortune,
Stroked with a knives tip,
Against her permission invaded,
Against her will impregnated,
And against her spirit,
Taken,
Held by devils,
Until her body received it,
First as her eyes spread water,
And then her head,
Until she became frozen like snow,
Melting to the ground,
For the devils fled then,
Terrified,
Like a ghost had haunted them,
The supernatural spirit,
For they had all seen her there,
And they ran to tell those they knew,
For they found the crystals when they returned,
Taking the crystals,
The crystals would become so cold,
That to touch a crystal would freeze skin from the hand,
The devils fled again,
And in more numbers still they returned,
Through one haunting night,
From the sky, it began to snow,

Beyond Devastation

Lost in a shadow land, of rocks, air without steam,
Hot sunlight, and barren houses,
Underneath, walking onwards,
Footsteps, breathing,
From such desolation,
The sun sets, red and ten times its size,
The setting light on the clouds,
For five hours through the darkness,
Until the heat of the day fades,
And coldness begins,
The lifelessness without changes,
A spiritual resonation begins,
For the few clouds that were,
Stars distantly,
The shadow land illuminated,
A half moon also,
Through coldness,
The sand and rock,
Through until a cave,
From such desolation, a passage,
To the sea, along the waterways,
The open ceiling,
Where dark skies are tinted with red,
And pink,
The silent shadow land,
Water for dehydration,
Through completion,
From the shadow of the body,
To the body with a shadow removed,
Sleeping in the moving water, cooler,
Between the end and a new beginning,

## Empowering

Obscure, without individual empowerment,
Apart of a system, systematic living,
Ignorance, believing the same,
Group empowerments,
Without that, despair,
Self destructive fear,
Phobic, avoiding it,
Individual empowerment,
The developed spirit,
Or, left to be impoverished,
Whatever fate there is to become,
With, or without truth,
Undeveloped resolutions,
Undeveloped belief foundations,
Overlooking the self,
Assuming alignments,
Self destruction,
Survival, or dissolution,
Truth or falsity,

Enlightened Awakening

Destined to obscurity,
Impoverished embodiments,
Resorting to spitefulness,
Perfection higher than divinity,
The use of a weapon,
The thieving of material,
Arrogant, violent,
Using weapons easily,
Disposing,
Abusive ranking,
Targeting,
Mysterious authority,
Rising,
Injury,
Fatal fatalism,
Covert,
Life for life,
Death for death,
Lost,
Mysteriously,
Evil empowerment,
True resolution,
Knowing truth,
Knowing falsity,
Ascended consciousness,

## Inner Peacefulness

What is the perfect form of the spirit?
Bound to some pattern of industry,
Acceptable among those local,
Within expectations,
Opinions,
Family,
Without that,
A spiraling failure,
Captivated by defeat,
Begging the opposition,
Violent ending,
What is the perfect form of the spirit?
From the awareness of the non human...
That is the cradle of divinity,
Empowering,
For thy effort thy attainment,
Apart of divinity,
Separate from material definitions,
From destruction new creation,
Separate from failure,
For like a seasons creations,
Aware of the winter,
Relief and fulfilling...

## Sensuality Storm

He held her, dainty, salacious, snug, and raunchy in his arms,
In a saturated cerulean and blush gown,
Walking through the submerged sand, through a storm,
In the crystalline, dark, cloud reflecting ocean water,
Explosive, booming, discharging, rumbling,
Thunder and lightning,
Dancing, flaring, flashing, shimmering,
Rainfall on the ocean waves,
She held on around his neck,
But she was laughing because she knew,
He would have her in the storms waves for a rascals prank,
As the lightning moved down to the earth,
Striking and making a crackling sound,
She would shriek softly,
Under the billions of raindrops falling,
The water kept her up,
Interlocked... the intercourse... feeling... stroking....
A thunder boom followed the lightning's crackle,
He laughed... and so did she...
In spite of the storm,
They would make it,
The 'ah', and 'oh' noises from her open mouth,
Were silent in the crushing, broken waves,
Through the thrill seekers turbulent accomplishment,
Their woes, and upsets, relieved,
With her rounded, smooth hips against his determined embrace,
Her eyes opened and closed, and blinked,
High into the sky,
And he stroked her center, with a finger and his pink flower arrow
She reached it, for he flattered her pink with his finger tip so...

After the crush

Of his release and hers

In their intense and high

Sensual forms

The Feminine Resolution

On a bed of rose thorns,
It seemed,
As she moved,
Her heart bled,
And she seemed in pain,
Sweating,
The heat of the Vietnamese sun beams,
Fading pink petals shrouded her body,
Absorbing her hearts power,
From the center, swarming,
The creative meditation,
Her divine form,
From her body, water and blood,
As though it were so,
For her glaring eyes were sharpened,
And her breath, sudden and fast,
Peaking for a cloud like falling,
Arching,
Her body hidden under faded pink petals,
Swollen,
Sighing as though suffering,
Falling from the high,
Flash flood!!!
She was thankful...
It was so...

Violence

Your dragon like feature,
Big eyes,
Pointed, round lips,
And big teeth,
Feminine embodiment,
True spirit,
Resolve my contention,
I've been captured,
And your savior is my freedom,
So steal what you can,
Spiteful of me,
Hurtfully,
Take what you have to,
Violent empress,
Noticing what is beneath,
With your fingernails,
And your teeth,
Making me fear you,
So quick and violent,
You practice,
Challenging me to resent you,
But I can't let you win,
So you torture it,
Swelling and bruises,
Scratches, and abrasions,
Waiting until I'm so offended,
But I only would rise,
So you sought the cream,
I kept in the cupboard,
And you ate it,
But it was only me,
It made me upset,
So I had to crush you,
And rob you of the fortunes,
The lock the pearl,
I made you scream, and cry,
But you could not move,
I was too much,
And you were captive,
Your hands and fingers in my hair,
My mouth made you react,
Why did you come?
I kept taking it,
And there was nothing you could do,

Rape Fantasy

Sexy lady,
Why did you do it?
I once had a rape fantasy,
But what you did was far more than I ever asked for,
Five of you, one with a gun,
And two with ropes,
What were you and your few thinking?
You waited until I was feeling safe,
You put a steel collar on my neck with a chain,
So I reacted, to moan, and awe, stunned, and shy,
You removed everything with your mouths,
Vulnerable and nude,
It did not matter then, how attractive,
I was overwhelmed,
So, so…
Is that how it goes?
So offensive…
Public controversy,
Police after you five,
Arrest warrants out,
You interrogated it,
And took control of it,
My chest,
But you were careful not to,
Make it happen to quick,
I was enslaved,
None of you concerned…
Exploiting and objectifying it,
Laughing with it,
Using it,
No human rights,
Criminal, unlawful,
Unequal,
Bitch,
Make me come again!

Capsaicin

It hurt so much,
Until you sucked my lip,
Swollen from the pain,
My hand was bruised,
My arm was tired,
You bit those places,
Just enough,
So that I felt the sting...
When you sucked my tongue,
And made it bleed...
Just a drop,
Like a hungry animal...
You would begin to bite,
The side of my belly,
Until your teeth were almost,
Leaving a red mark...
For whatever defeats I have had,
Fallen sensations,
Destructive durations,
You had to relieve it...
With your mouth,
Biting my shoulder,
Making pain,
So that you could taste,
My wounded skin,
Sighing when I'm moaning...
My ear lobe... making me cringe...
Taking me out into the cold,
Riding it until I cannot keep my love within...
You spanked my bare chest, until it was pink,
Sucking and biting my skin...
Tasting my pain,
So that you would know,
Giving in...
You would spill your love,
With me in the wet dirt...
You would laugh,
And relax...
And you would rest on my chest,
So I would take my opportunity,
To make you react...
Too intense...
My offering...
For what you could give...

Alluring The True Alignments

With your breast to my mouth,
I will have your bosoms peak,
The point of creative celestial empowerment...
Look to the stars,
As you feel the delight,
Swelling within the chest,
Beloved breasts...
Beneath, above, beside...
My hands... and my tongue...
Creation celestial in your heart,
The rhythm of truth,
Where my fingers venture,
You cannot...
For your hand surrounds my hand,
Pulsing until you feel higher,
Two fingers,
Up and down...
Soft and hard...
Your sigh so refined,
Softest feminine,
Most feminine feminine...
Until you are so high,
That you cry...
I cannot stop,
I will do anything...
I will make your heart too fast...
And make drops of sweat fall from your neck...
Together...
We can ascend the truth,
Until we are two sweat soaked bodies bound...
To each other, bare and content...
Pure, and clear...
Our environment will only resonate,
Of our intense pleasure,
Happiness, sorrow, and fear,
With you wrapping me in your embodiment,
There should be no sooner end than later...
A lasting kiss to relieve the highest enduring...
The latest snow and ice we shared...
The divine love to... in the pleasure release...

Southeastern Sensuality Royal

Surround me with your following,

Let them see how I pleasure her...
Her legs apart...

In the center of your following,

So they would know,
Swaying as one...
Wooing her cries,
With my leg between hers...
With her breast in my hand...
And my tongue in her mouth,
" Ooh," they would react,
For them to absorb,
The intense motion,
To hold her leg raised,
She would moan "ah", drawn out...
And again, and again,
However savage,
"Uh," drawn out... "Ah," drawn out...
And she wept...
As she began to release,
Over the flat stone open grounds,
The stream...
"Ah, ah," louder, faster...
Until she received the divine esoteric offering,
From within, I prolonged her poses,
And her followers received the sensations,
Continuing...
I relieved her with my fingers,
Spilling over the flat stone open grounds,
Her followings intense and vivid respires,
I took her over me,
On the flat stone open grounds,
To receive the divine esoteric offering again,
As from her center more saturating elixir spilled,
For the fortune of our pursuit,
Among her surrounding feminine adhering,
Applause and rejoice...
Through deep grey and stormy clouds,
The suns mysterious steam light glowing, sparkling beams,
A warming visage through the skies, to earth,
Rain circles through the air surrounding the openings in the clouds,
Surrounded by the green paradise of her incarnate heritage...
Reflected in their swerve eyes, the ancient preserving of their earth...

Vietnamese

However the wind may seem to move...
Whatever destiny may seem to come...

You should know the truth

The truth beyond assuming...
For resting and considering...

The truth beyond
Is how to know
What is what
In the divine form

Creation... preservation... destruction...

And eternity...

For there is refinement
Efficiency, wastefulness

The sources...
To know...

Provides perceptions of beyond

Subtle sensations
The third eye
Beloved form
Attracting thy

Consider me a brother and father...
Know what I intend...
And the spiritualities of reality...
The true forms...
So that you shall ascend...
Accept true celestial energy to yourself...
Resolve mistaken will and choices...

For all destruction and creation does vary
Know how to refine thy progress
Thy balance

And know how to recognize true authority...

Beloved

The Great Goddess, aligned with Hindu supreme goddess, the Mahadevi by Aeon Julian

With darker lighting to indicate the completion

Notes About The Author

The photo was self taken, during the spring break holiday in 2003, in Utah, at the age of 14, inside of my grandparents van. I'm a natural redhead During the early 1990's I went on many hikes in Utah, Colorado, and Arizona, with my grandparents, mother, and those several month pursuits were spiritually significant. (A blue lens was used to create double eye color in the photo)

My birthday is October 23, 1988. I was born in Ireland, living there for ten years from birth. My mother is American German, Cajun French, Scottish, Danish, Italian, English and Welsh and Irish.

Aeon is a self given name. The family given name remains confidential for personal preference.

I have lived in Galway Ireland, Atlanta Georgia, Austin Texas, Charlottesville Virginia, Chicago Illinois, and currently reside in Los Angeles California.

I have family and friend connections in Louisiana. Due to many holidays there, in the 1990's, it became like a second home to Ireland

I abstain from drinking and smoking and pursue faithful enlightenment, independently from religious associations, with most significant observance of Hindu and Buddhist teachings.

I currently have another literary project, a realistic and spiritual space fantasy novel, which is already in the second draft stage of development, inspired by the most epic spiritual, science fiction movies in recent movie history.

Other long term pursuits include music, some of which is available on iTunes and other music networks. And currently, massage therapy, and alternative body building.

Warning